C000101913

MAKE AND COLOUR

Under the SEA

Clare Beaton

b small publishing

How to use this book

First remove the centre black and white pages of the book. These are sea creatures and plants for you to colour in.

Place the book on a flat surface and ask an adult to help you open the staples. Carefully pull out the centre black and white pages, then close the staples again.

First colour the outlined shapes. Use coloured pencils, crayons, felt-tip pens or paints. See below for painting suggestions.

Keep the rest of the book. It has lots of ideas on how to make seascapes and aquaria in which to hang your cut-outs. You will also find many fishy facts about the sea creatures on the inside back cover.

Some things you will need:
- coloured paper and tissue paper
- cardboard tubes, boxes, and egg-boxes
- plastic bags
- scissors, craft knife
- tracing paper, pencil, ruler
- sticky tape, glue
- crayons, paints and felt-tip pens
- sequins and glitter
- darning needle and thread
- wire coat-hangers

This symbol is to remind you to ask an adult to help when you use a craft knife.

Paint effects

Use fairly thick paint and wash your brush between colours. Leave the pages flat to dry, then cut out the shapes.

Paint patterns
Paint the shapes with watery paint. While they are still wet, use thicker paint in contrasting colours to add spots or stripes.

Glitter
Make glittery patterns on coloured paper or painted shapes. Draw patterns in glue, then shake glitter over them. Pour the excess glitter off.

Sea stripes
Paint stripes using watery paint. While it is still wet, add the next stripe in another colour so that the colours run together.

2

Templates

Here is a way to trace simply and successfully from the templates on the inside front cover and page 6.

What you will need:
○ tracing paper
○ soft pencil
○ sticky tape
○ paper or card

1

Tape a piece of tracing paper over the template. Trace the shape with the pencil.

2

Turn over the tracing paper and scribble over the lines with the pencil.

3

Turn over again and tape on to some card or paper. Retrace firmly over the lines. Remove the tracing paper.

Stencils

Cut or tear off the sheet of stencils from the back cover. Follow the instructions below on how to use them.

What you will need:
○ paper or card (coloured if you want)
○ pencil
○ scissors

1

Place the stencil shape on the card or paper. Draw inside the shape with a pencil.

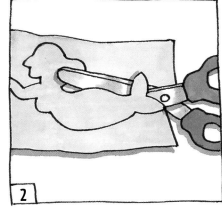

2

Colour in the outline shape or cut it out with scissors and make a mobile (see page 8).

Special seascapes

Cut the flaps off one end of a cardboard box. Keep the card flaps. Tape up the other end to make the box stronger.

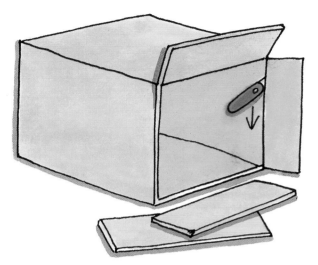

Cut off about one third of the box.

Paint the inside of the box: make the sides greeny blue and the bottom sandy yellow.

Warm southern seas
Coral reef, turquoise sea, yellow sand, brightly coloured fish.

Cold northern seas
Greeny blue sea, wreck on brownish sand, seaweed, dull coloured fish.

Colour the seaweed and corals from the centre pages, and glue them inside the box.

4

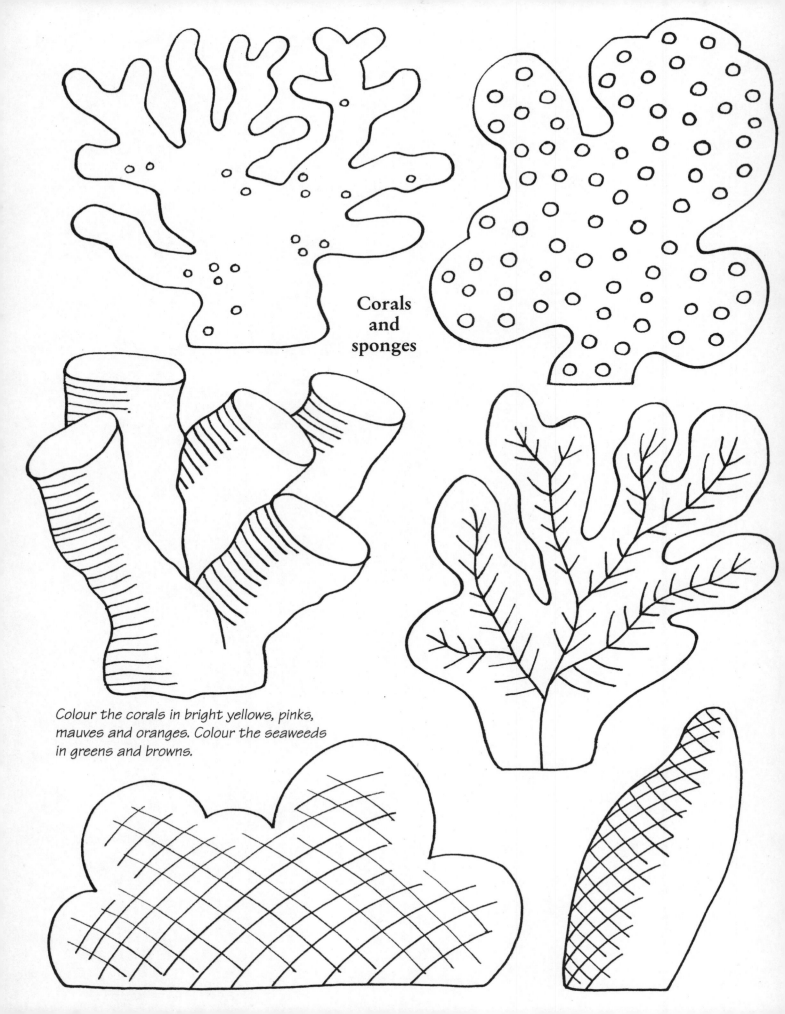

Corals
and
sponges

Colour the corals in bright yellows, pinks,
mauves and oranges. Colour the seaweeds
in greens and browns.

Hermit crab

Swordfish

Turtle

Sea slug

Sea cucumber

Sea snail

Electric eel

Angel fish

Sharks

Piranha

Common sunstar

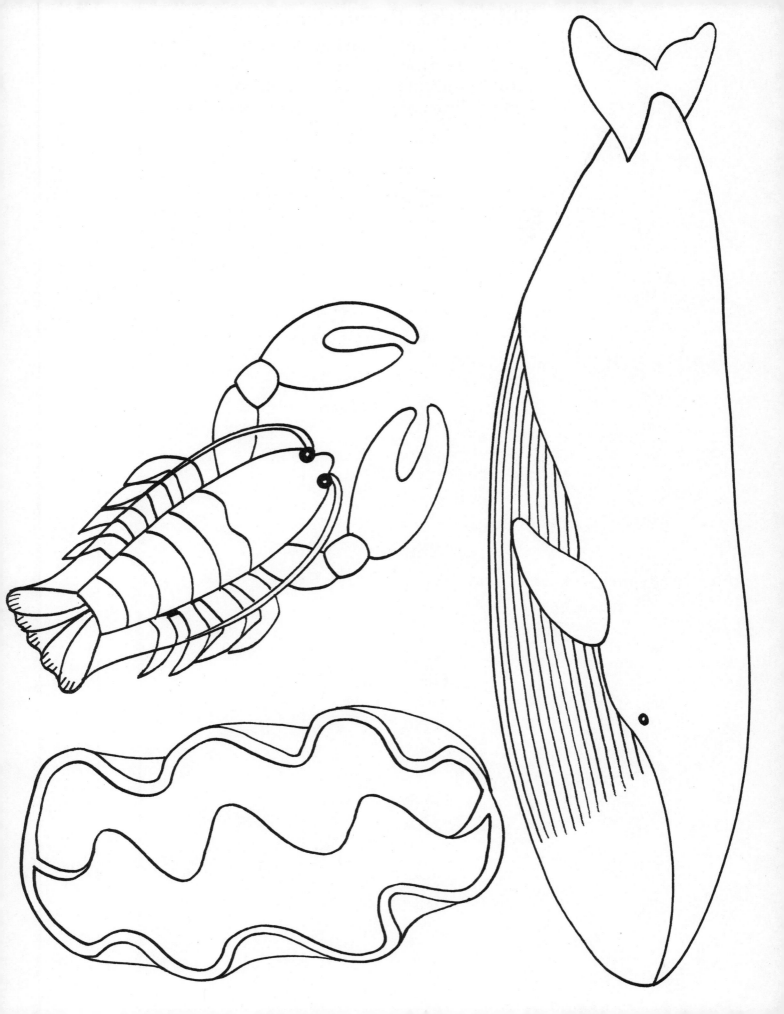

Things that live under the sea

Colour in the shapes on both sides, then cut them out.
Look at the painting ideas on page 2 before you begin.
Don't worry if you paint over the edge, remember
you will be cutting out the shapes afterwards.

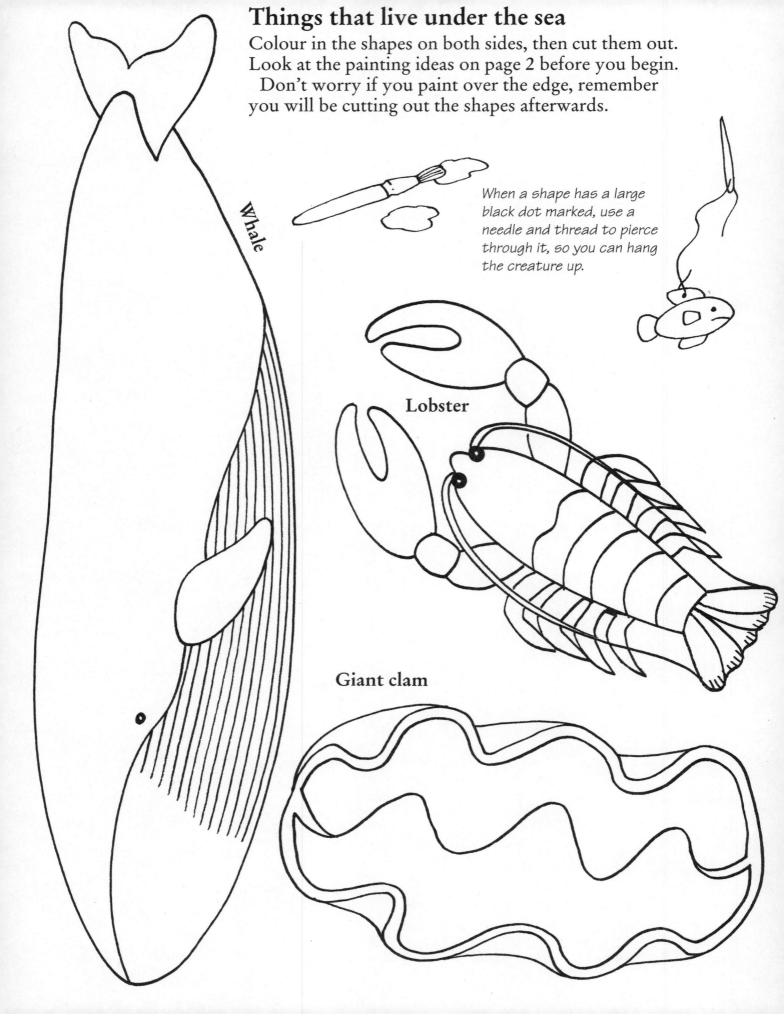

Whale

When a shape has a large black dot marked, use a needle and thread to pierce through it, so you can hang the creature up.

Lobster

Giant clam

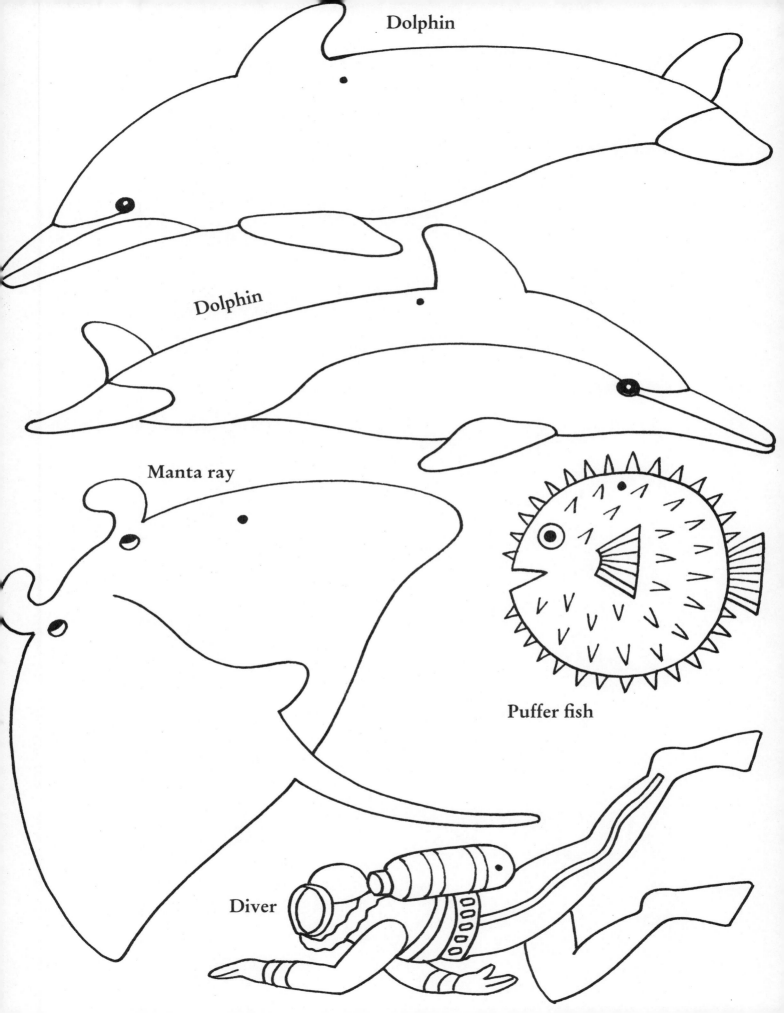

Dolphin

Dolphin

Manta ray

Puffer fish

Diver

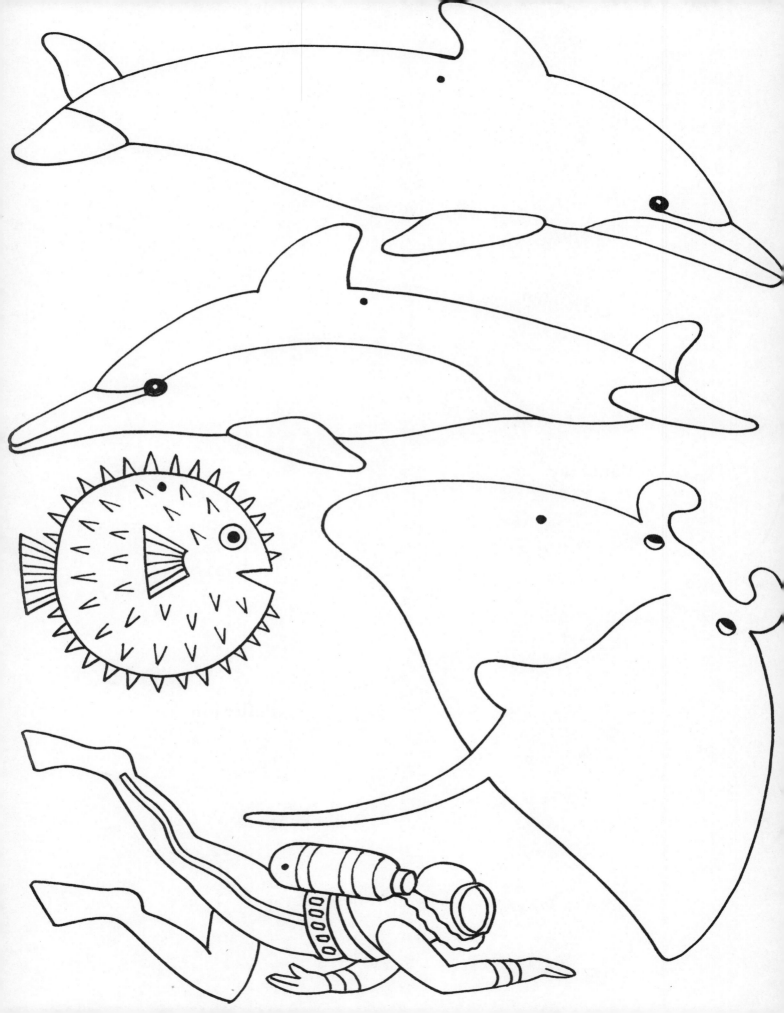

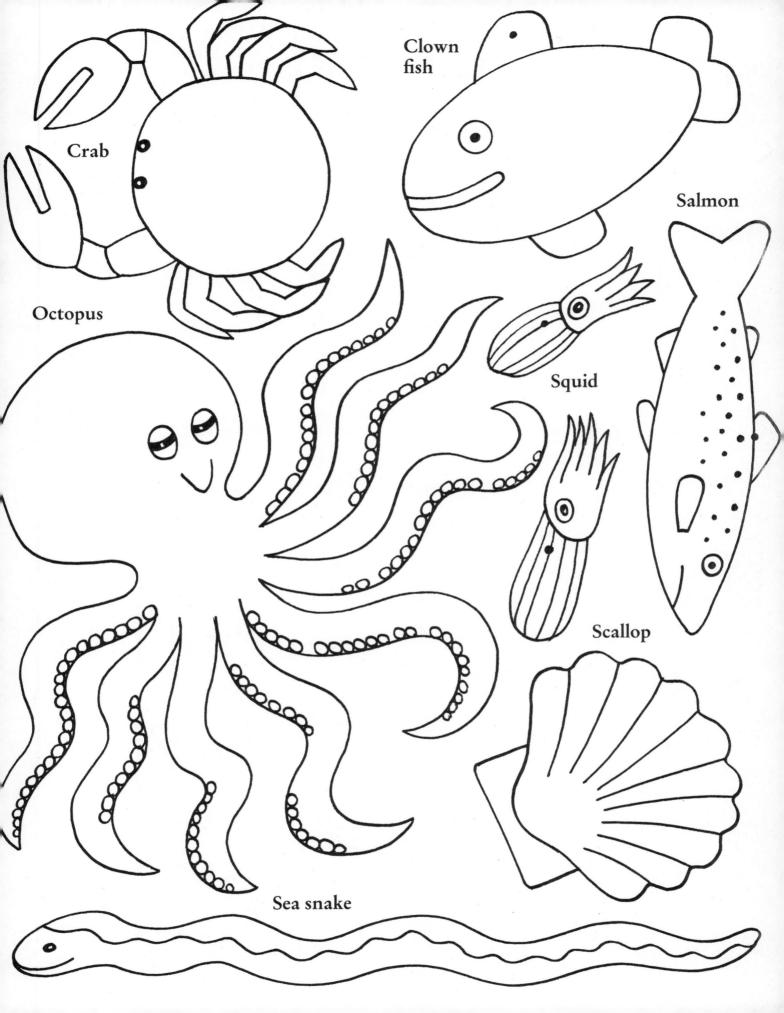

Crab

Clown fish

Salmon

Octopus

Squid

Scallop

Sea snake

Starfish

Shrimp

Tropical fish

Seahorse

Shrimp

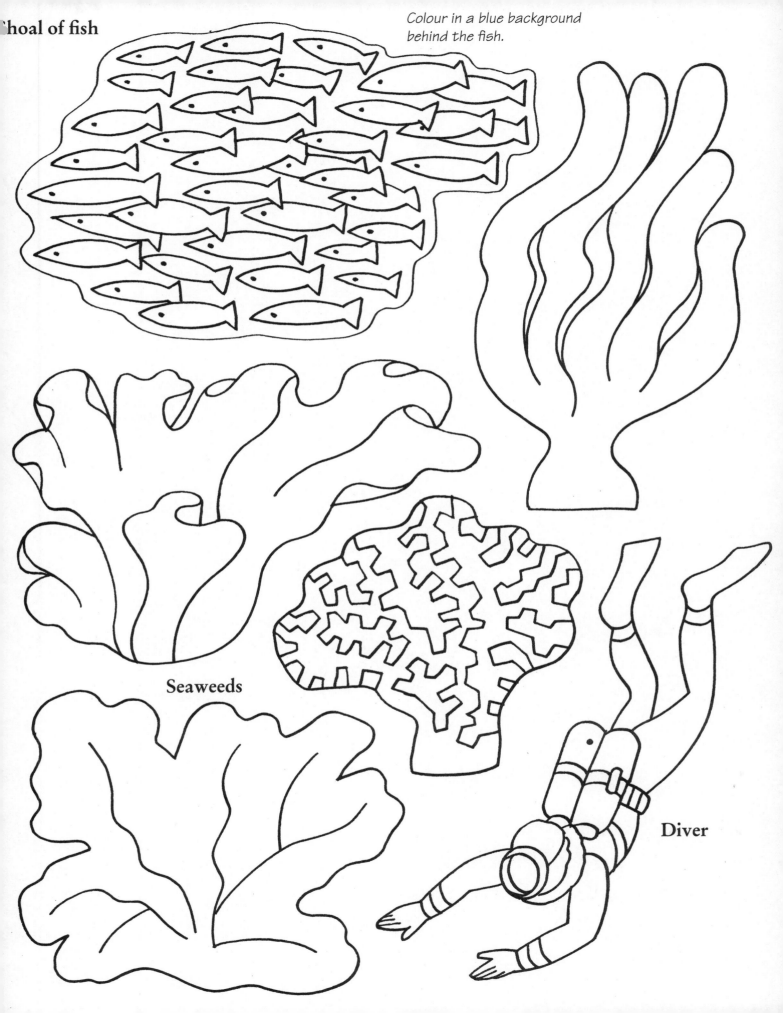

Shoal of fish

Colour in a blue background behind the fish.

Seaweeds

Diver

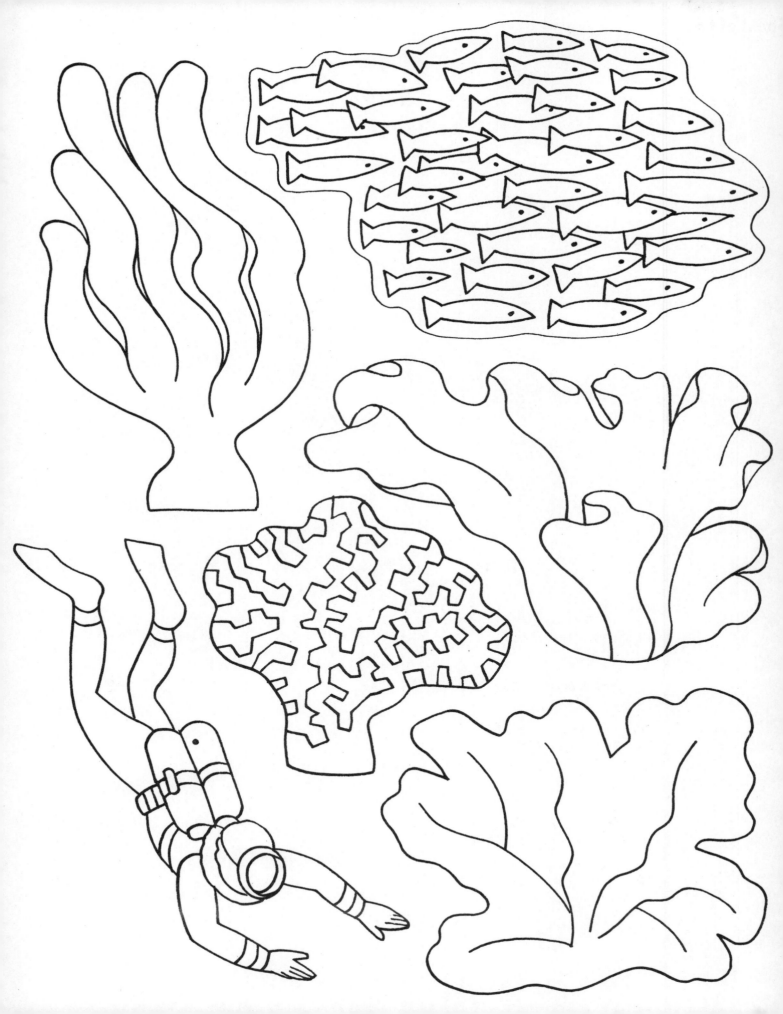

Decorate and cut out some of the fishy creatures on the centre pages. Tie threads of different lengths to them. Use a darning needle to push the end of each thread through the top of the box. Knot and tape down the ends. Cover and decorate the outside of the box.

Sea anemone

Paint a 6-cm length of card tube, inside and out. Cut a fringe to half-way down the tube. Bend the fringe down. Place your anemone on the sand.

Wreck

Use one cardboard flap to make the ribbed remains of a ship.

Cut the card with a craft knife, as shown below. Paint it dark brown on both sides. When dry, bend up the ribs. It doesn't have to be too neat.

Jellyfish

Cut one of the small cups from an egg-box. Trim it.

Cut a clear plastic bag or some tissue paper into narrow strips.

Tape the ends of the strips inside the cup. Push some thread through the top with a darning needle. Tape or knot the thread inside. Hang up.

5

Amazing aquaria

These are really fun to make, and they look great.

Make them as colourful and sparkly as you can.

glitter

shiny paper

sequins

foil sweet wrappers

Tissue box aquarium

Cut the top of an empty tissue box into an uneven shape. Paint the outside of the box.

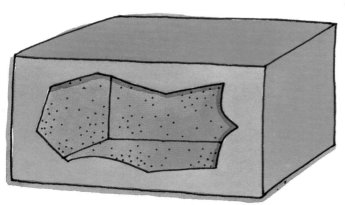

Paint the inside of the box bright blue, and leave it to dry. Then dab patches of glue around the inside, and pour in some glitter.

Shake the box to spread the glitter over the glue. Empty out any excess.

Use the templates below to cut out lots of little fish from coloured foils. (See page 3 for how to use templates.)

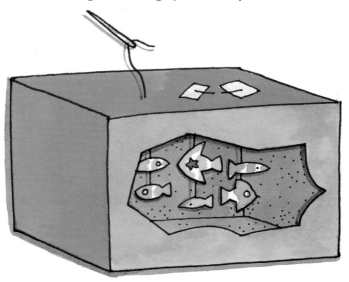

Glue or tape the fish on to some thread.

Use a darning needle to thread the fishy strings through the top of the box. Tape down the ends.

Next use the stencils to cut out shapes in coloured foils and paper.

6

Glue the shapes on the outside of the box. Add glitter and sequins.

There are lots of pens available for different special effects. Perhaps you could buy one or two.

Matchbox aquarium

Remove the sleeve from a large matchbox. Cut a hole in the top.

Paint the inside of the box drawer bright blue. Paint fronds of weed.

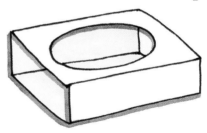

Cut tiny fish out of bright-coloured paper or foils and glue them on the back.
  Push the sleeve on to the drawer.

Decorate the box with small real or drawn shells. Fill in the gaps with lots of glue. Then sprinkle on glitter. Shake off any excess.

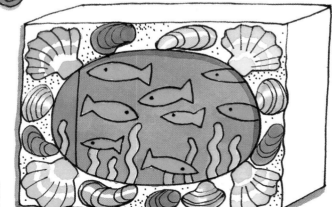

7

Marine mobiles

Use the stencils to make lots of coloured paper shapes for a mobile. If you need help, see the stencil instructions on page 3.

Decorate the shapes on both sides with sequins, sticky shapes or pens.

Attach a length of thread to each shape, using a darning needle.

Choose a bright-coloured wire or plastic coat-hanger. Attach the shapes to the hanger.

Cut blue, green, and white plastic bags into thin strips and glue or tape them on to the hanger, between the fishy shapes.

Flying fish mobile

Use the template inside the front cover to make a fish body out of stiff paper.

See page 3 for how to use a template.

Use a craft knife to cut the slot marked on the template. Decorate the fish body brightly on both sides.

Take a double thickness of tissue paper about 25 cm x 15 cm. Fold it into a fan 3 cm wide.

Push the fan through the slot and fold it upwards. Glue where the two sides touch.

Tape a length of thread inside the fan to hang it up. Open the fan downwards to make two 'wings'.